RYE FREE READING ROOM

A Treasure at Sea for DRAGON and Me

Water Safety for Kids (and DRAGONS)

Written by Jean E. Pendziwol

Illustrated by Martine Gourbault

Kids Can Press

One hot summer day at the end of last week,
My good friend the dragon came up from the creek.

Dad waved at the dragon, then leaned down to say,
"Let's pack up a picnic and go to the bay."

"I can swim," I told Dragon as Dad went to pack;
"I've had lessons. Can you swim?" He nodded "Yes!" back.

We put on our swimsuits, our sunscreen and hats,
And packed my red wagon with towels and mats.

With shovels and pails, the dragon's bear, too,
And my nifty spyglass, we'd have oodles to do.

When we got to the beach, we took shovels in hand
And raced off together to build in the sand

A castle with turrets, a dungeon and moat,
A sea monster, shark and a four-masted boat.

"Hey, Dragon," I said, with a wink of an eye,
"There's pirates about! Did you see them sail by?"

I jumped up and snarled, feeling rough, tough and bold,
"Let's follow those pirates and capture their gold!"

The dragon was eager to join in the fun,
So he sprang from the sand and he started to run.

With a leap and a bound and a dragon-sized hop,
He was into the water before I yelled "STOP!"

"Hey, matey," I said, "Even pirates can't swim
Till Dad comes and says it's okay to go in."

Dad looked in the water and checked the beach sands,
For rocks, glass or tins that could hurt feet or hands.

I flourished my spyglass up to my eye,
Scanned the horizon, inspected the sky.

"Captain," I said. "It's calm and it's clear,
There's a lifeguard on duty, we've nothing to fear."

Dad gave the okay; then making a dash,
My buddy and I went right in with a splash.

The dragon stretched out like a great pirate ship,
And I grabbed his tail by its very green tip.

"Ahoy, mate," I sneered, "Could that dock be their lair?
Let's check if that scurvy crew left treasure there."

But no loot was found, though we searched every spot,
Not a coin nor a gem from that unruly lot.

"Well, keelhaul the crew! Let's watch where they go,
Then check in the water for treasure below."

We climbed on the dock and I sat looking out;
Then I noticed my buddy and let out a shout!

The dragon stood poised and was ready to leap,
But he hadn't checked first if the water was deep.

"Dragon! Don't jump! It's shallow!" I said,
"Don't dive off this dock or you might hurt your head!

Instead, you landlubber, watch this! Look at me!"
And walking the plank, I stepped into the sea.

Waving at Dad and then plugging my nose,
I turned upside down and I waved with my toes.

I surfaced again for a quick breath of air,
Then dove to the bottom to look for loot there.

When I came up again, to my great dismay,
The dragon was heading out into the bay!

He'd crossed the buoyed line to where deep water flows,
And all I could see was his tail and his nose.

He was chasing a pirate ship right out to sea,
But I knew that my buddy should stay close to *me*.

"Hey, Dragon!" I hollered, and Dad hollered, too,
But he couldn't hear us … A shrill whistle blew!

The lifeguard swam out. A rescue at sea!
She brought that big dragon back safely to me.

"The water out there is way over your head;
Swim here with your buddy, it's safer," she said.

My poor friend the dragon, his head hung in shame,
Hiccupped then sneezed (all smoke and no flame).

"It's okay," I told him. "You're safe now, you're fine.
Let's go back and swim but stay inside the line."

We splashed in the water, two pirates at sea,
Swimming together, the dragon and me.

Then my heart skipped a beat — you'd never guess why —
A note in a bottle was bobbing close by!

Could it be? Do you think? Would it tell us the way?
Could there really be treasure somewhere in this bay?

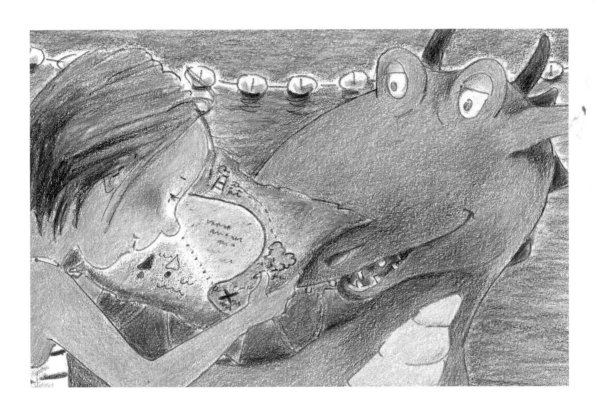

I pulled out the cork and the paper inside.
It was a MAP! I opened it wide.

It showed the whole bay, as clear as could be,
The dock and the beach and the twisted old tree.

"Up anchor! Set sail! Let's head for the beach,
A treasure is buried close by, within reach!"

But scuttle the scuppers, we ran out of luck;
Our ship ran aground in the seaweed and muck.

I stepped overboard and ran down its length,
Then leaned on the stern with all of my strength.

I pushed and I shoved and I pushed a bit more,
Till I'd shoved that big dragon up onto the shore.

"By Jove and by Jimmy (and by Jenny, too),
Let's rescue the loot from that mutinous crew!"

We followed the clues leading in from the sea,
Then up from the beach and around the old tree.

Two swashbuckling pirates, all sandy and hot,
We finally stopped over *X marks the spot.*

A treasure of crackers, cheese and cold meat,
Lemonade, pears and a sweet chocolate treat.

Pirates we are, an unruly bunch,
But even a pirate gets hungry for lunch.

The Dragon's Water Safety Rhyme

STOP! It's exciting to go for a swim,
But think of these rules before you get in.

LOOK! Is a grown-up close by and in sight?
Is the water calm and the weather all right?

Read all warning signs. What do they say?
Is there anything sharp that might be in your way?

Before you dive in, is it deep down below?
LISTEN to lifeguards and always GO SLOW!

If you've got the okay, it's time to get in,
Take your buddy along and be safe when you swim!

The dragon now knows some important water safety rules, and children will pick up many water safety tips as they follow the dragon and little girl through *A Treasure at Sea for Dragon and Me*. Point out the rules, and put them into action the next time you go to the pool or beach. You may even want to have a treasure hunt of your own!

The most important rule, however, is not for dragons or children. As parents and guardians, you are responsible for being alert when children are playing in or near water — any water. They need the full attention of an adult who is watching, listening and ready to help if need be.

Here is a checklist to discuss and put into action together:

● Always get adult permission before going into *any* water, whether it's a bathtub, pool, hot tub or lake, and make sure there is adult supervision.

● It's important for everyone to know how to swim. Take lessons in swimming and water safety from a qualified instructor.

● All children should learn to do basic water rescues, and all teens and adults should also learn basic lifesaving techniques.

● Inner tubes, water wings, air mattresses and even life jackets are not substitutes for adult supervision. Young children who do not know how to swim should be within arm's reach of an adult at all times — whether or not they are using swimming aids.

● The dragon has a buddy. Do you? Stay close to your buddy.

● Check out the swimming area before going into the water. Look for signs that may give information about currents, tides or other hazards, and observe weather markers such as flags. Check to see if there is a lifeguard on duty. Make sure the weather is good and the water calm, and be alert to any changes. Never swim when thunderstorms are in the area. If other people are using the area for waterskiing, personal watercraft or boating, choose a safer place to swim.

● Never, ever dive into water before checking first to find out how deep it is. You need at least 2 m (6 ft.) of water for safe shallow diving. If in doubt, wade in or jump in feet first.

● If you see someone who needs help, tell a lifeguard or an adult right away. Don't go in to help, but do throw the person a flotation device, such as a life ring. If there is an emergency and lifeguards are on duty, know the whistle signals they use and obey them. If in doubt — get out!

● Remember to be sun safe by putting on sunscreen, wearing a hat and sunglasses and drinking lots of water.

● When in a boat, always put on and fasten your government-approved PFD (Personal Flotation Device). Make sure that it is the right size for your weight. Remember, PFDs only work when you wear them!

● Stay off of frozen lakes, ponds, rivers and streams until an adult checks to make sure the ice is safe. Ice should be at least 20 cm (8 in.) thick for a group to safely walk or skate on. The moving water of rivers and streams freezes more slowly and thaws more quickly than the still water of lakes and ponds.

● Learn the dragon's water safety rhyme and be water safe!

To my favorite paddling pirates and beach buddies,
James, Karol, Zachary, Stuart and Anna — J.E.P.

To Sacha P. — M.G.

With thanks to Jean Hall-Armstrong, lifeguard extraordinaire.

Text © 2005 Jean E. Pendziwol
Illustrations © 2005 Martine Gourbault

All rights reserved. No part of this publication may be reproduced, stored in
a retrieval system or transmitted, in any form or by any means, without the
prior written permission of Kids Can Press Ltd. or, in case of photocopying
or other reprographic copying, a license from The Canadian Copyright
Licensing Agency (Access Copyright). For an Access Copyright license,
visit www.accesscopyright.ca or call toll free to 1-800-893-5777.

Kids Can Press acknowledges the financial support of the Government of
Ontario, through the Ontario Media Development Corporation's Ontario
Book Initiative; the Ontario Arts Council; the Canada Council for the Arts;
and the Government of Canada, through the BPIDP, for our publishing
activity.

Published in Canada by	Published in the U.S. by
Kids Can Press Ltd.	Kids Can Press Ltd.
29 Birch Avenue	2250 Military Road
Toronto, ON M4V 1E2	Tonawanda, NY 14150

www.kidscanpress.com

The artwork in this book was rendered in pencil crayon.
The text is set in Berkeley.

Edited by Debbie Rogosin
Designed by Karen Powers

Printed and bound in China

The hardcover edition of this book is smyth sewn casebound.
The paperback edition of this book is limp sewn with a drawn-on cover.

CM 05 0 9 8 7 6 5 4 3 2 1
CM PA 05 0 9 8 7 6 5 4 3 2 1

National Library of Canada Cataloguing in Publication Data

Pendziwol, Jean E.
    Treasure at sea for dragon and me : water safety for kids (and dragons) /
written by Jean E. Pendziwol ; illustrated by Martine Gourbault.

ISBN 1-55337-721-4 (bound).   ISBN 1-55337-880-6 (pbk.)

1. Aquatic sports — Safety measures — Juvenile literature.
I. Gourbault, Martine II. Title.

GV770.6.P44 2004   j797.2'0028'9   C2004-903113

Kids Can Press is a *Corus*™ Entertainment company

JUL 1 3 2005

RYE FREE READING ROOM
1061 BOSTON POST ROAD
RYE, NY 10580
(914) 967-0480

LC 4/14/21 = 60X R 6/25